Cambridge **Discovery Education**™

▶ **INTERACTIVE READERS**

Series editor: Bob Hastings

FOUND
DISCOVERY AND RECOVERY

B1

Brian Sargent

CAMBRIDGE UNIVERSITY PRESS
Cambridge, New York, Melbourne, Madrid, Cape Town,
Singapore, São Paulo, Delhi, Mexico City

Cambridge University Press
32 Avenue of the Americas, New York, NY 10013-2473, USA

www.cambridge.org
Information on this title: www.cambridge.org/9781107632127

First published 2014
Reprinted 2014

Printed in Hong Kong, China, by Golden Cup Printing Company Limited

A catalog record for this publication is available from the British Library.

Library of Congress Cataloging-in-Publication Data

Sargent, Brian, 1969-
  Found : discovery and recovery / Brian Sargent.
    pages cm. -- (Cambridge discovery interactive readers)
  ISBN 978-1-107-63212-7 (pbk. : alk. paper)
1. Lost articles--Juvenile literature. 2. Personal belongings--Juvenile literature. 3. English
language--Textbooks for foreign speakers. 4. Readers (Elementary) I. Title.

AM501.L67S37 2013
081--dc23

                              2013014260

ISBN 978-1-107-632127

Additional resources for this publication at www.cambridge.org

Layout services, art direction, book design, and photo research: Q2ABillSMITH GROUP
Editorial services: Hyphen S.A.
Audio production: CityVox, New York
Video production: Q2ABillSMITH GROUP

Contents

Before You Read:
Get Ready!

Read the paragraph. Then complete the sentences with the correct highlighted words.

There are many treasures, or valuable things, buried below the surface of the earth. Coal and other minerals can be found there. To get them, people sometimes dig tunnels under the ground. These tunnels can collapse, or fall down, hurting or killing the people inside.

1 The boy built a bridge with his toys, but the wind made it

_____ .

2 The man found an old coin _____ in his backyard.

3 Gold, silver, and copper are examples of _____ .

4 _____ is often burned for heat and power.

5 When it's cold, the _____ of the ground is hard so it's difficult to dig a hole.

6 Deep in the cave, the children found the king's hidden

_____ .

Words to Know

Match each profession with its description.

_____ **1** emperor

_____ **2** warrior

_____ **3** researcher

a a person who fights in a war

b the male ruler of an empire

c a person who studies a subject to learn more about it

Words to Know

Use the words in the boxes to complete the paragraphs.

endangered	rare	searched

1 The scientist **a** _____ for many days until he found what he was looking for: the giant panda. Giant pandas are an **b** _____ species and in danger of dying out. The scientist was very happy to see this **c** _____ and unusual animal.

characteristics	genes	genetics

2 **a** _____ make living things the way they are. They are found in living cells. In humans, genes are passed from parents to children. They decide our skin, eye, and hair color, as well as other **b** _____. The study of genes is called **c** _____.

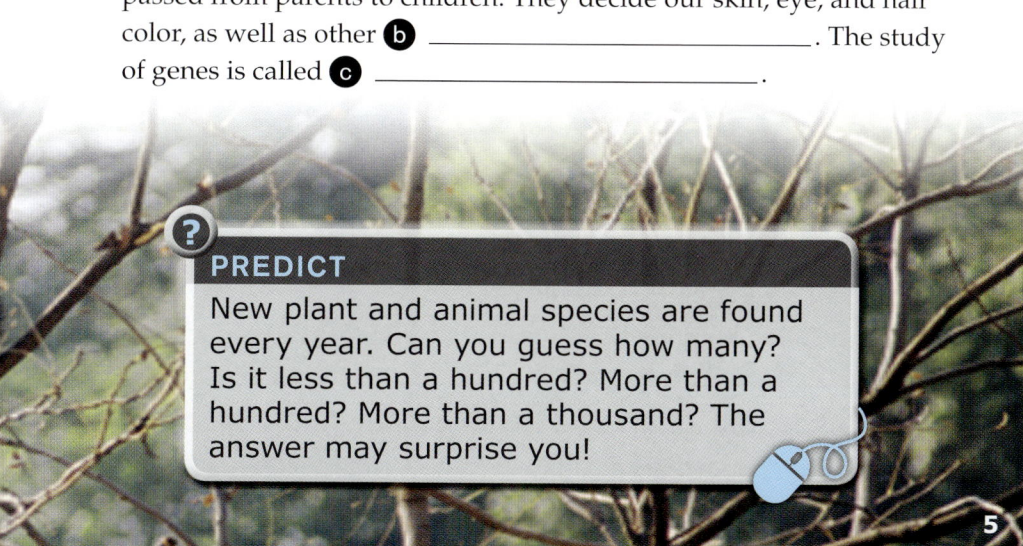

? PREDICT

New plant and animal species are found every year. Can you guess how many? Is it less than a hundred? More than a hundred? More than a thousand? The answer may surprise you!

CHAPTER 1

Found (and Lost)

WORKERS FIND A 60-YEAR-OLD UNOPENED LOVE LETTER. WHEN THEY RETURN IT, WILL THE COUPLE STILL BE IN LOVE?

In 1952, Dick Hauck and his girlfriend Arlene wrote many love letters to each other. Dick was far away, serving in the US Army, and Arlene was home in Minnesota. They wrote every day. Then Dick wrote the most important letter of them all. He sent it on March 31, 1952. Arlene didn't get it until 60 years later.

In the letter, Dick asked Arlene to marry him.

Workers found the letter in 2012. They were fixing the home where Arlene grew up when they **discovered** the unopened letter hidden underneath a part of the floor. Instead of throwing the old letter away, they used the name and address on the envelope to find Arlene and deliver it to her. The good news is Dick and Arlene had gotten married anyway. They are still married today.

There are many different things you can find. Like the workers in this story, you can find something that was lost. You can find your keys or your cellphone hidden under the seat on your car. You can also find things that were not lost, but haven't been discovered yet. You can find a new species of fish living deep under the water. You can find the cure[1] for an illness or a new medicine to help people feel better.

You can find out something. "To find something out" means to discover or learn new knowledge. For example, you can find out that you like swimming after years of being afraid of the water.

You can also find the time or find the energy to do something you have always wanted to do.

What else can you find? Read this book and find out!

[1] **cure:** something that makes someone with an illness healthy again

CHAPTER 2

Aha!

IN 2006, ALMOST 17,000 NEW ANIMALS AND PLANTS WERE FOUND. THAT'S ALMOST 50 A DAY!

There is something very unusual living deep in the high mountains of Myanmar, the country formerly called Burma. It is a monkey that sneezes[2] when it rains. The monkey has almost no nose, and when water runs down its face, it sneezes it away. Have you heard of it? Probably not. Nobody had heard of it before 2010. That's when the monkey was found for the first time.

Every year, an amazing number of new plant and animal species are found. Modern ways of collecting and **identifying** living things allow scientists to find more new species than ever before. Some say we are in a "Golden Age of Discovery." To show this, scientists at the University of Arizona counted the number of new plants and animals found only in 2006. The number? 16,969!

[2]**sneeze:** When you sneeze, air comes out through your nose and mouth.

About half of the new animals found in 2006 were insects. In addition, researchers counted 2,000 new plants. Mammals[3] were less common. They made up about 1 percent of the new species.

One reason for the high number of new species is transportation.[4] Modern transportation allows researchers to travel to new areas that had been difficult to visit and search in the past. The sneezing monkey is an example of a new species found because researchers were able to go deeper into forests and higher into mountains than ever before.

[3] **mammal:** an animal that feeds its babies with milk from its body
[4] **transportation:** something such as buses, cars, or trains, used for getting people or things from one place to another

Another reason for the high number of newly discovered species is genetics. Genetic testing tells us more than other methods of identification. For example, scientists used genetic testing on a common type of butterfly called the skipper butterfly. They learned that this butterfly was actually made up of ten different species of butterfly. From the outside, the butterflies all looked identical, or exactly the same, but the genes showed differences. Testing showed that each different species had its own characteristics and history.

In a similar study, a group of scientists tested a collection of 730 known birds and bats. To their surprise, they discovered 21 new species in the collection. Each new species looked the same as a known species. The differences only appeared when they studied the genes of the animals.

New species aren't the only things you can find with genetic testing.

A skipper butterfly

EVALUATE

Explain the idea that we are in a "Golden Age of Discovery."

In 2008, a New York City high school became partners with the American Museum of Natural History to help students learn more about the city by using genetic testing. That year, two students collected fish from markets around New York City. When they tested each fish, they found that one quarter of the fish sold in the markets was labeled incorrectly. In most cases, a cheaper fish was given the label, or name, (and price!) of a more expensive fish. The two students also found that some markets sold endangered fish labeled as other fish.

fish

A year later, two more high school students used genetic testing to find out what animals they could find in and around their New York City apartments. They collected over 200 animals from their apartments and neighborhoods. From the collection, they identified 95 species, including a new kind of cockroach never identified before.

cockroach

CHAPTER 3

Unearthed

CHINESE FARMERS FIND A 2,000-YEAR-OLD ARMY WAITING UNDER THE GROUND.

For 2,000 years, a huge[5] army waited east of Xi'an, in China. It had thousands of soldiers: some were sitting around or cooking on small fires; others were taking care of farm animals or horses dressed for war. Most of the soldiers, however, were standing straight and holding weapons.[6] There were rows and rows of them, standing and waiting, ready to fight. But they were all below the ground.

In 1974, their long wait ended. A group of farmers were digging a deep well to get water when they found pieces of the army. The army was made of terracotta, a kind of clay, or soft earth. It had been built for Ying Zheng, the first emperor of China. As a child, Ying Zheng became king of Qin, a state of modern-day China. He took the name Qin Shihuangdi. At the time, Qin was at war with the six other states of China.

[5] **huge:** very large
[6] **weapon:** something dangerous that you use in a fight, like a gun or knife

The army was made of terracotta.

Qin Shihuangdi's armies brought the states together to form the nation of China.

To protect[7] him after death, Qin Shihuangdi had a new army of 8,000 terracotta warriors made. The figures were life-sized and very realistic. They were also secret. Some people say the emperor killed anyone who worked on the terracotta soldiers or knew the **location** of the underground army.

It took 2,000 years, but the army was found. Some of the warriors, like the ones found by the farmers, were broken, but many were still whole. Now the soldiers themselves live the life of emperors. Some travel the world, from museum to museum. The rest stay in China. They live in a giant museum, still standing in great, long lines. People around the world know about Qin's terracotta warriors.

[7]**protect:** keep someone or something safe from something dangerous or bad

Treasures from past civilizations[8] aren't the only **valuable** things **buried** under the earth. For thousands of years, people have worked hard to dig coal and minerals out of the ground. This is called mining.

Gold mines can be found in 25 countries around the world. Gold is also one of the oldest minerals mined from the earth. Around 6,000 years ago, the Ancient Egyptians mined for gold in the area now known as Nubia. Gold from this region was used to create some of the ancient[9] world's most beautiful works of art.

The oldest mine in the world is far older than the gold mines of Nubia. Somewhere between 40,000 and 80,000 years ago, early people mined a mineral called specularite in the Lion Cavern in Swaziland, Africa. Specularite is a silver and blue rock that shines in the light. Researchers believe the people living there used the specularite as makeup.

[8]**civilization:** a society or group of people living together at a certain time
[9]**ancient:** very old

Video Quest

Giant Trucks

Watch this video to learn about giant mining trucks. How wide is Bingham Canyon?

Today, there are two main types of mines: underground mines and surface mines. Underground mines are usually tunnels dug deep into the ground. Working in these tunnels can be very dangerous. Deep underground, the air can sometimes be very unhealthy, and miners can be hurt, trapped,[10] or killed when tunnels collapse.

Surface mining is less dangerous to miners, but not to the earth. Surface mines dig away the plants and other life on top of the ground so miners can reach the minerals below. Surface mines can be very, very large. In some cases, whole mountains are dug up to get the valuable minerals underneath.

[10]**trapped:** when you cannot move or cannot leave a place

CHAPTER 4

Looking for Loot

**IT IS EASY TO LOSE THINGS IN THE OCEAN.
FINDING THEM AGAIN IS FAR MORE DIFFICULT.**

In 1554, four ships set out from Mexico to Spain. They were led by Captain Antonio Corzo and were full of treasure. For over 60 years, Spanish conquistadors[11] had taken incredible amounts of gold and silver from the many people and rich gold mines of North and South America. Captain Corzo's ships were filled with such **loot**, including about one million gold coins. Some say his ships were the richest treasure ships to ever travel over the sea.

Less than three weeks later, three of the four ships were lost in a storm off the coast of Texas. Many people were killed, and the treasure sank to the bottom of the sea.

[11] **conquistador:** one of the Spanish soldiers who traveled to North and South America starting in the late 15th century

Stories like this are common. In fact, there are so many stories of lost treasure in the sea, you might think the whole sea floor is covered in shining gold. However, the sea is an amazingly big place, and finding anything there is a rare and lucky event. That doesn't stop people from trying, though.

Salvage companies are groups that travel around the world and look for lost ocean treasure. Often they use sonar[12] to look for sunken ships on the sea floor. Then, they send divers down to explore the area. Some companies even use machines to explore the area first. Most of the time, salvage trips return with nothing. Other times, the things they find are not very valuable. However, in some trips salvage companies find something truly amazing.

[12] **sonar:** something that uses sound waves to find the location of things in the water

[13] **automatic lifeguard:** a lifeguard machine, a machine that works by itself or with little human control, that makes sure that people who swim are safe from danger

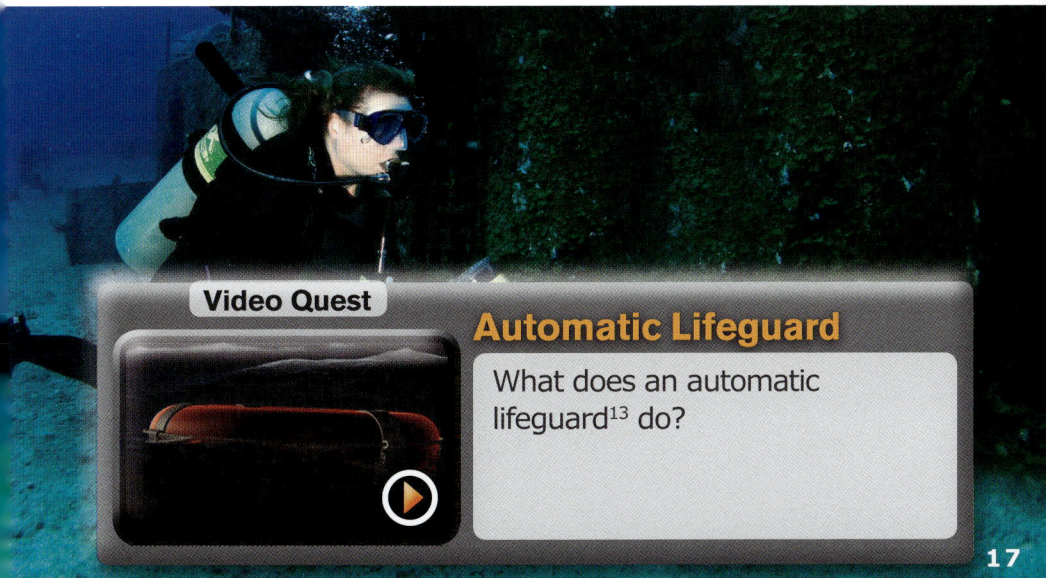

Video Quest

Automatic Lifeguard

What does an automatic lifeguard[13] do?

One lucky find happened in 2007, when a salvage company found something unusual near Gibraltar, Spain: $500 million worth of silver and gold coins. It was an unbelievable find.

There was one problem, though. No one could tell from what ship the coins had come. There were very few pieces of the ship left, and none of the pieces were big enough to help identify it. This was important, because the name of the ship would decide what happened to the treasure. International law says if a salvaged ship is a private[14] ship, then the salvage company can keep anything it finds. However, if the ship is a government ship, then the ship and everything inside it still belongs to that government. It was very important to find out what ship these coins had come from.

....

[14] **private:** owned by a person or company and not by the government

Spain said the ship was the *Nuestra Señora de las Mercedes*, a government ship which left Peru for Spain in 1804. International courts [15] agreed and ordered the salvage company to give the coins to the Spanish government. The salvage company disagreed, but there was little they could do. They had found one of the most valuable treasures under the sea, but they could not keep it.

Although most ocean treasures sink, that doesn't mean you can't find interesting things on the ocean's surface. In 2012, a New Zealand ship found something very strange on the surface of the ocean. There were millions of rocks **floating** on the water, like a huge shelf covering 26,000 square kilometers. That's as big as the country of Haiti! The rocks were a volcanic stone called pumice, which is lighter than water.

[15] **court:** the place where a judge makes a decision based on law

Pumice sometimes comes out of a volcano.

A radio telescope

CHAPTER 5

Eye in the Sky

DO YOU HAVE A COMPUTER? IF YOU DO, YOU CAN TAKE PART IN ONE OF THE BIGGEST SEARCHES IN HISTORY.

As long as people have looked to the stars, they've wondered if there was life up there. An organization called Search for Extraterrestrial Intelligence (SETI) aims to answer that question. SETI uses modern technology to search the skies for some sign of extraterrestrial life, or life on other planets. One way they do this is by listening for radio signals[16] from other planets. SETI uses a large number of radio telescopes to collect information from space. Then, using computers, they look through the information for signals.

So far, SETI has found no signs of extraterrestrial life. However, they have searched only a small number of available radio waves. To make the search go faster, SETI invited ordinary people around the world to help them.

[16]**signal:** a series of sound waves that carry information

An optical (regular) telescope

They invented SETI at Home, a computer program that uses home computers to search through collected information. When SETI invented the program, they hoped to have between 50,000 and 100,000 owners of home computers help them. By 2011, over a million computers from more than 200 countries had joined in the search.

William Herschel did not have the help of a million computers when he searched the sky. He didn't even have one. What he had instead was his sister, Caroline. Together, before his death in 1822, they had found and mapped more than 90,000 stars.

William Herschel

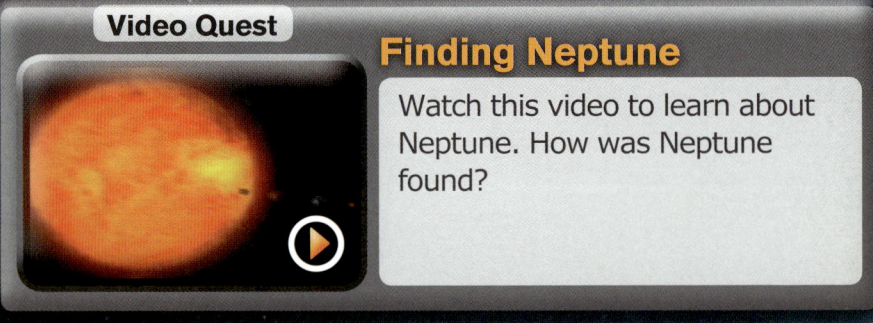

Finding Neptune

Watch this video to learn about Neptune. How was Neptune found?

Herschel, a British **astronomer** born in Germany in 1738, spent hours in his workshop, building mirrors for his telescope. Herschel wanted to find stars that appeared close together. Herschel hoped measuring[17] the distance between these stars would show how fast the stars were moving. However, over time, he noticed some groups of stars that were not behaving as he expected.

Herschel had discovered double stars. These were stars, he learned, that were caught in each other's **gravity**. Because of this they turned or **orbited** around each other. In total, Herschel discovered over 800 double or multiple star systems. While searching for these star systems, Herschel made another important discovery: Uranus, the seventh planet from our sun.

....

[17] **measure:** find out how big, long, heavy, or fast something is

Uranus is made mostly of gas, but can you imagine a planet made from diamonds? Astronomers in 2011 may have discovered one. The planet moves extremely fast, orbiting its star every two hours, and astronomers believe that it used to be part of a double star.

When two stars are close together, like double stars, something interesting can take place. Astronomers call it mass transfer, and it happens when one star pulls away the mass[18] of the second star. In the case of the diamond planet, which goes by the less interesting name of PSR J1719-1438, the second star pulled away much of the original star's mass, leaving behind a large amount of carbon.[19] Astronomers believe gravity and heat caused the carbon to form a diamond.

....

[18] **mass:** a large body of matter with no shape

[19] **carbon:** the small pieces of matter that form together to make diamonds

CHAPTER 6

What Do You Think?

1. At a market in Pennsylvania, USA, a man bought a painting for four dollars. The painting was not very good and had a large hole in it, but the man didn't mind. He bought it because he liked the frame[20] around the painting.

When he got home, he pulled off the old painting and found a small, folded[21] piece of paper hidden behind the frame. The paper was an original copy of the US Declaration of Independence. It was printed on July 4, 1776, the date of America's independence from Britain. Only 23 copies were known to exist. This one made 24.

A year later the man sold the copy for just over $2.4 million.

[20] **frame:** the thing that goes around a painting, usually made of wood

[21] **fold:** If you fold paper, you bend it so that one part of it lies flat on top of another.

2. Jeff Bidelman was helping a family clean out an old house. Nobody had lived in the house for 20 years. The family had asked Bidelman to help look through it for anything valuable.

Upstairs, Bidelman found a small hole in a wall. He asked the family about it. A woman who had lived in the house as a girl told him an old family rumor.[22] "The woman said when she was a kid, there were always rumors that that's where they threw money," Bidelman later said.

When he went downstairs, he found out the rumor was true. On the bottom floor, Bidelman found $100,000 worth of old, valuable coins inside the wall below the hole.

....

[22] **rumor:** something a lot of people talk about, although they do not know whether it is true

After You Read

Read the sentences and choose Ⓐ (True) or Ⓑ (False).

1 Some rocks can float.

Ⓐ True
Ⓑ False

2 You can keep any treasure you find on the ocean floor.

Ⓐ True
Ⓑ False

3 Unhealthy air is one problem faced by underground miners.

Ⓐ True
Ⓑ False

4 Valuable things can sometimes be found in surprising places.

Ⓐ True
Ⓑ False

Match

Choose the best match for each sentence.

1 I read books to _____ about new things.

2 John needs more sleep to _____ to do his big project.

3 Susan works long hours and can never _____ to watch TV.

ⓐ find the time

ⓑ find out

ⓒ find the energy

Choose the Correct Answers

Read the following sentences and choose Ⓐ, Ⓑ, Ⓒ, or Ⓓ.

1 The sneezing monkey sneezes in the rain because _____.

  Ⓐ it lives in the mountains of Myanmar
  Ⓑ it was found in 2012
  Ⓒ it has no nose
  Ⓓ it has no mouth

2 Genetic testing is useful in finding _____.

  Ⓐ underwater loot
  Ⓑ new species
  Ⓒ lost love letters
  Ⓓ rare coins

3 Collapsing tunnels is a problem for _____.

  Ⓐ surface mining
  Ⓑ underground mining
  Ⓒ underwater salvaging
  Ⓓ underwater robots

4 SETI is searching for _____.

  Ⓐ signals from extraterrestrial life
  Ⓑ double stars
  Ⓒ new planets
  Ⓓ diamond planets

?

EVALUATE

When the high school students used genetic testing on fish sold around New York City, they found many markets were selling one type of fish while calling it another. Why might the markets be doing this?

Answer Key

Words to Know, page 4

1 collapse **2** buried **3** minerals **4** Coal **5** surface
6 treasures

Words to Know, page 5

1 b **2** a **3** c

Words to Know, page 5

1 Ⓐ searched Ⓑ endangered Ⓒ rare
2 Ⓐ Genes Ⓑ characteristics Ⓒ genetics

Predict, page 5   There are thousands of new species found each year.

Analyze, page 7   She was too busy.

Evaluate, page 10   *Answers will vary.*

Video Quest, page 14
Bingham Canyon is four kilometers wide.

Video Quest, page 17
It helps save people who are in danger in the water.

Video Quest, page 22
A French astronomer used math to locate Neptune.

True or False, page 26

1 A **2** B **3** A **4** A

Match, page 26

1 b **2** c **3** a

Choose the Correct Answers, page 27

1 C **2** B **3** B **4** A

Evaluate, page 27   *Answers will vary*